Community Volunteers

by Cam Gregory

Focus Points
Community

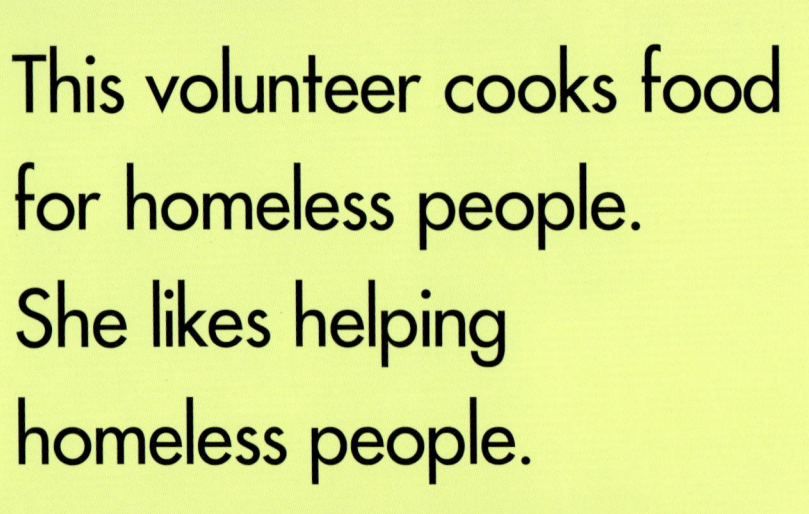

This volunteer cooks food for homeless people. She likes helping homeless people.

2

This volunteer brings food to an old man's house.

These volunteers grow food to share with people. They like sharing the food they grow.

6

This volunteer takes an old lady to the shopping mall.

8

This volunteer takes a disabled person for a walk.

This volunteer makes quilts to keep people warm.

These volunteers knit clothes for needy children.

These volunteers collect clothes.